There is no evidence of any settlement in Poole's Old Town Peninsula during the Roman period, even though the neighbouring area of Hamworthy was already an established port. The development of Poole seems to have been much later. It is not mentioned in the Domesday Book of 1086, and it was not until the thirteenth and fourteenth centuries that Poole really began to establish itself as an important trading centre.

The importance and growth of Poole during this period was probably due to two things: first, the silting up of the deep water channel to Wareham, which forced shipping to seek other landing sites; and secondly, Poole's gradual independence from the Manor of Canford.

Poole's first step toward independence from Canford was the Longspee Charter granted to the town in return for 70 marks in 1248 by William Longspee, the Lord of the Manor of Canford. The Longspee Charter gave the townsfolk the right to elect six burgesses to form a Borough Council, one of whom would be selected by the Lord of the Manor to preside as Port Reeve. This released Poole from the direct control of the Lord of the Manor of Canford and gave it greater freedom in its self-government and development.

By the end of tl ... beginning to
establish itself as an ... l kinds. The
town was still small ... zed between
the quay on the on ... n the other.
There was in fact a v ... ing the early
medieval period, Poc ... nassive tidal
bog sweeping arou ... ...dge is now,
through to Parkstone Bay. And the harbour line was quite different from what we see today.

Then, the quayside was little more than a sandy beach running away from the line of Strand Street. The word "Strand" means shore and Poole's Strand Street - like London's more famous Strand - was once beside the water, with jetties providing landing stages.

These jetties were later built up to form the curious set of lanes between Strand Street and the modern quay, such as Buttons Lane, Bull Lane, and Ball Lane, but in the early medieval period they provided the town with secure landing stages.

These may seem primitive facilities today, but part of Poole's attraction for shipping was that the town was generally safe from attack. It was protected on the landward side by the huge tidal bog, and its approach by sea was difficult for those who did not know the harbour, with shallow water barely covering treacherous mudbanks upon which a ship could easily become stuck fast. Although the quayside facilities were undoubtedly primitive, the town's safety as a harbour quickly attracted shipping of all kinds.

Unfortunately, and despite the harbour's natural defences, the town also attracted the unwelcome attention of raiders from across the Channel. Poole - along with Melcombe Regis and Lyme Regis - was raided by the formidable French Admiral Jean de Vienne in 1377, and later by a joint Franco-Spanish fleet in 1405. This later raid was probably in retribution for the raids on northern France and the coast of Spain by Harry Paye, whose pirate fleet was based in Poole between about 1402 and 1405 - and whose brother was killed in the raid of 1405.

By the sixteenth century, Poole's status as the most significant trading port in Dorset was assured, and the Great Charter granted to the town by Elizabeth I in 1568 created "the County of the Town of Poole, distinct and separate from the County of Dorset."

But if the activities of the raiders were not particularly conducive to the growth of the town during the medieval period, the Royal Charter of 1433, which established Poole as a Port of the Staple, certainly was. This Charter, which gave Poole the authority to collect customs duties on behalf of the King, not only guaranteed Poole a very useful income from taxes on imported and exported goods, but also guaranteed the growth of the town during the late medieval period. Twenty years later, in 1453, Poole's economic prosperity was secured by a Charter from Henry VI allowing the town to hold a weekly fair and an annual market.

This independence and stability was soon to be disturbed by the Civil War (1642-1649). Although no major battles were fought in the County, Poole was clearly of strategic importance to both sides. Hit hard by Charles I's demands for Ship Money, Poole, in common with most seaports, was staunchly Parliamentarian from the outset, even though most of the County was inclined to the Royalists. After refusing to yield to the King's request for allegiance in 1642, Poole set about defending itself and in 1643 began its first assault on the Royalist stronghold of Corfe Castle.

This was quickly called off after the fall of Dorchester to the Royalists in the same year, and the town made itself ready for a lengthy siege. Following a carefully-laid plot by Captain Francis Sydenham of the Poole garrison in which Royalists, under the command of the Earl of Crawford, were lured into the town only to be ambushed, the town again seemed free from the threat of siege, the Royalists not wishing to venture too readily into the Parliamentarian Poole. Corfe Castle eventually fell to Parliamentarian forces in 1645. It was during this period of the Civil War that, according to local tradition, Oliver Cromwell stayed at Byngley House, his officers being stationed at Scaplen's Court.

Following the execution of Charles I in January 1649, the town's relationship with Parliament seems to have been a relatively peaceful one. But the restoration of Charles II to the throne in 1660 put the town in an awkward position. Parliamentarian and Protestant, the town now had to defer to the wishes of the Crown, and to the dictates of a Catholic King.

Some healing of the breach between Poole and the King was made in 1665, when Charles II visited the town and stayed at the house of Peter Hiley. The house, which was medieval in origin, was demolished in the 1960s, but a plaque now marks the spot where the house once stood. Nearby is a plaque identifying the spot where the Reverend John Wesley, grandfather of the founder of the Methodist Church, was imprisoned for about six months in 1665.

The King's visit to Poole paid some dividends, for in 1667 Charles II granted a new Charter to the town re-affirming the Great Charter of 1568 which had given Poole the status of a discrete County, theoretically independent of Dorset. But the relationship between Poole and Charles II was never a good one, and in 1683 - two years before his death - the King withdrew the privileges granted to the town by the various Royal Charters over the years.

The accession to the throne of the assertively Catholic James II must have concerned the town's leaders greatly, and they were surely relieved by the arrival of the Protestant William of Orange on the English throne in 1688. This gave Poole time to recover from its political position as an opponent of the old Royalists and to concentrate on strengthening its economic position. Throughout the eighteenth century, and running through into the early part of

the nineteenth century, Poole attracted considerable wealth by virtue of the Newfoundland trade, and many of its most impressive buildings date from this period.

This Newfoundland trade was firmly in the hands of a few families - families whose names are still held in considerable regard. These families - Spurrier, Jolliffe, Lester, Garland, Kemp - were responsible for the building of many of the outstanding examples of Georgian mansions and civic buildings in the town during the period, and are commemorated at various points around the town.

Most of these families have some interesting historical connections with the town. The most famous is probably that of Captain Peter Jolliffe. The Jolliffe family was already distinguished in Poole by the seventeenth century when, in 1694, Peter Jolliffe captured and eventually wrecked a French privateer

off the Lulworth coast. He was rewarded with a gold medal from William of Orange, and the deed is commemorated in an inscription in St James's Church which tells how Jolliffe "signalised himself against the French.... and frequently revenged their insolences towards the English by captivity or death".

Another of the great Newfoundland trading families - the Spurriers - has a quite different history. Christopher Spurrier was responsible for the building in the early part of the nineteenth century of Upton House, which is now owned by the Borough Council with protective National Trust Covenants, and is open to the public. But the family's history is a sorry story of prominence and wealth, followed only by bankruptcy and degradation.

In the early part of the eighteenth century, the family amassed a tremendous fortune through the Newfoundland trade and a series of judicious marriages into both the Jolliffe and Garland families.

Upton House: looks across at Poole from the far side of the Holes Bay shallows.

But following a series of disastrous fishing seasons at the Newfoundland trade, the family fell into bankruptcy in 1830, and never recovered its former status in the town. Christopher Spurrier, bankrupted and separated from his wife at the age of 47, lived until he was 93, and was buried in obscurity.

The wealth brought into the town by the Newfoundland trade came to a fairly abrupt end in the first half of the nineteenth century, following the effects both of the American War of Independence - after which America monopolised the Newfoundland fishing trade - and also the ending of the Napoleonic Wars in 1815, which brought the French back into merchant trading. By the middle of the nineteenth century, Poole's Newfoundland trade was a thing of the past, and so too, was the wealth associated with it.

Ironically, Poole regained some of its earlier status through the growth of its neighbour, Bournemouth.

Bournemouth was little more than a muddy creek before the nineteenth century, its only visitor the occasional smuggler. But by the 1850s Bournemouth's population exceeded 5,000. These new inhabitants all had to be housed, and this stimulated a new economic prosperity in Poole. During the latter half of the nineteenth century, the town produced, handled and supplied massive quantities of building materials, out of which was constructed Bournemouth, that "fairy palace suddenly created by the stroke of a wand, and allowed to get a little dusty", as Hardy calls it.

This new trade changed the shape of Poole considerably. The town expanded out into Longfleet, Newtown, Branksome and Parkstone, just as more recently the town has spread out into Oakdale and Canford Heath. Most of the splendid Georgian and medieval mansion-houses were divided into tenements to house the dock-workers and their families, and the old town became once again the working port it had been in the medieval period.

Following a rash of demolition in the early 1960s, which destroyed many houses of real historic and architectural interest, a planned attempt was made to preserve some of the town's medieval and Georgian heritage, centering on the old town around St James's Church

The Guildhall was renovated and opened as one of the town's museums in 1972, followed by the Woolhouse or Town Cellars, similarly renovated and opened as the town's Maritime Museum in 1977. More recently, Scaplen's Court, originally a medieval town house but separated into tenements sometime at the end of the last century, has been refurbished and now serves as another of the town's three excellent museums, all of which must be visited to appreciate better Poole's history. There is no doubt that the preservation of the Old Town has been carried out with the utmost care and attention to detail.

But much more, inevitably, has been lost, and replaced with buildings of little architectural merit or imagination.

Poole is no longer what it was, but we hope that your walk around the old town will give you some idea of the town's history, and some idea, too, of the people whose lives shaped its history.

THE TRAIL

Scaplen's Court - later tenements stripped to
reveal mediaeval stonework. Drawn by Sheila Sturdy.

The walk starts from the **Hill Street** multi-storey car park, which is signposted from Towngate roundabout. Turn right out of the car park main entrance, and take the first turning on the left marked **Carters Lane.**

This takes you into the **High Street** where you turn right. Cross the main road after about fifty yards, carrying straight ahead into the continuation of High Street. On your left about twenty paces from the main road crossing High Street you will notice the **King Charles Memorial Plaque**, commemorating Charles II's visit to the town in 1665.

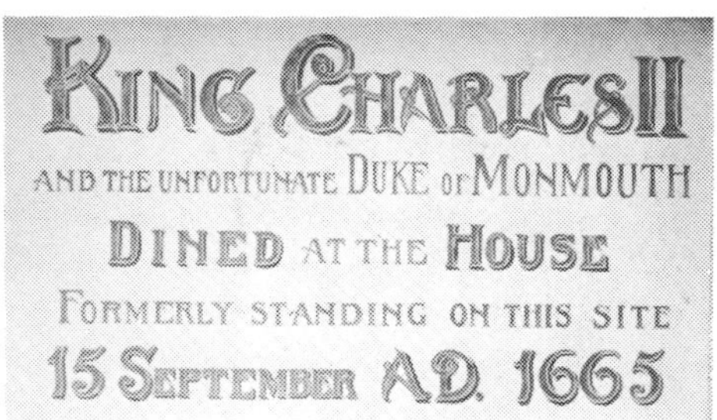

Continue on down High Street taking the first turning on your right into **New Street**. After about thirty yards, turn left into **Cinnamon Lane**. Stop at the rear of **14 High Street**, which is just before you reach the Antelope Hotel.

Here you will see the facade of a Tudor building, uncovered

during demolition. The building is characteristic of the early Tudor period: close timber-framed, with a slight overhang on the first storey and carved scrollwork decorating the barge-boards to the gable-end. This facade is indicative of Poole's relationship with the past. Discovered accidentally, it shows that much of Poole's history is hidden away from view, and has to be quite deliberately searched out. It is this hidden history which we hope to be showing you on your walk around the Old Town.

Continue to the end of Cinnamon Lane and turn left into the alley immediately before the rear of the Antelope Hotel. At the end of the alley turn right into High Street.

On your right is the **Antelope Hotel**. This fine old coaching inn dates from the

Antelope Hotel - with the beast mounted above the bay-window. The brick frontage is 18th century but inside there are older fireplaces and beams. Once it had its own brewery.

sixteenth century, although much of the facade is an eighteenth-century addition. Inside, however, exposed ceiling beams and two sixteenth century fireplaces recall its history. In the eighteenth century, the Antelope's own brewery stood conveniently next door.

Mail coaches, stage coaches and carriers left from the inn each day. Pigot's Directory of 1830, for example, records: "To Bath and Bristol, from the Old Antelope Inn, the Wellington Coach departs every Tuesday, Thursday and Saturday morning at half past six; goes thro' Wimborne, Blandford, Shaftesbury, Gillingham, Stourhead, & co." Nineteenth-century travellers made early starts!

About thirty yards on the right after the Antelope Hotel you will see **Scaplen's Court.**

A visitor to Poole in the early part of this century would have seen of Scaplen's Court only a dull tenement building. Then during a great storm in October 1923 a chimney crashed down, demolishing part of the fabric of the house. A long period of restoration revealed what the modern visitor now sees: a splendid example of a quayside home of the late medieval period.

The building dates from the late fifteenth century. It is constructed primarily of Purbeck stone, from the opposite side of

Scaplen's Court - a 1923 rediscovery, now restored as a mediaeval townhouse.

Poole Harbour, although there are also many cobbles in the walls; these are not local, and it is probable that they were spare material carried as ballast by ships visiting Poole at the time, and used by a thrifty medieval builder.

John Leland, the antiquary, visited Poole in the mid sixteenth century, and describes "a fair town house by the kay". He may have been describing this building, which must have been one of the finest houses of its day. Part of the building's original grandeur is indicated by the fact that it once served as the Town Hall, where, according to the Constitution of Poole of 1567, the City Fathers "weekly upon the Thursday betwene the houres of viii or ix of the clocke in the fournone mete and assemble themselves at the towne house there to debate of such things as shal be mete and convenient ".

Between 1642 and 1646, during the Civil War, it seems likely that Roundhead troops were stationed in the building during the sieges of the Royalist Corfe Castle. Many of their initials and dates are carved into the old stone fireplace as permanent graffiti!

The building was used as an inn during the seventeenth century, until bought for his private use by John Scaplen in the eighteenth century.

Like others of the town's museums, Scaplen's Court is a credit to Poole's Museum Department and you'll gain a real sense of the atmosphere of past times from visiting the house.

The interior has been restored in the style of a medieval town house, and the fine old fireplaces are particularly striking. The kitchen has been equipped with utensils and furniture of the Victorian/Edwardian period.

Continue straight ahead with Scaplen's Court on your right. You are now walking towards the **King Charles Inn**. The King Charles is one of the oldest public houses in the town. It was built towards the end of the sixteenth century, but was considerably altered in the nineteenth century, although some of its Tudor characteristics have recently been restored. In the 1890's the building, despite its age, was known as the New Inn, but the Charles connection predates this modernisation.

Local tradition has it that the building was re-named the King Charles in 1665, the year in which the restored King, Charles II, visited the town. It is more likely, however, that the

King Charles Inn - when it was the (not so) New Inn.

connection with King Charles refers to a French rather than an English king.

In 1830, the exiled Charles X of France landed at Poole on the Hamworthy side of the quay. Following the fall of Napoleon at Waterloo in 1815, France had returned to monarchic rule under Louis XVIII and then Charles X. But both Kings had been unpopular and civil revolution forced Charles X to leave his country. He crossed the Channel, originally intending to land at Spithead. But he was denied a landing there because of intense anti-French feeling and was transferred to a British naval steamship. The ship landed at Poole, but the King, afraid of anti-French feeling in Poole also, put in on the Hamworthy side, from where he was quickly escorted to Lulworth Castle, the

Thames Street - which has broken through the west end of the Woolhouse or Town Cellars. This building of about the 1430s has superb mediaeval timber roofing and is now a magnificent period setting for the town's Maritime Museum.

home of the Catholic Weld family.

At the King Charles Inn turn left towards Poole Quay into **Thames Street**.

Immediately on your left as you leave Thames Street is the **Woolhouse** or **Town Cellars**, now the town's **Maritime Museum.** As its name implies, The Woolhouse was built as a warehouse for storing wool and cloth ready for export. It was probably built in the early fifteenth century, about the time that Poole was created a Port of the Staple (1433), although a stone building of some type had existed on the site from about 1300, or even earlier.

The Woolhouse, with its fine collar and tie beam roof, is a remarkable example of medieval architecture, and is probably the oldest building in the town. It was originally about 150 feet long, but was cut in two sometime early in the nineteenth century when Thames Street was extended to give easier access to the Quay. The other half of the building still survives, and can be made out behind the brick facade of what is now part of the King Charles Inn, on the opposite side of Thames Street. This - the **King's Hall** - has recently been annexed to the King Charles, although it is probably more than a hundred years older than the King Charles itself, and was originally a part of the Woolhouse.

The eastern portion of the Woolhouse was refurbished in 1977 and now houses the town's excellent Maritime Museum. Permanent exhibits of boats, maps and accounts illustrate the town's shipping connections, and particularly the Newfoundland trade.

At this point on the quayside you will see also the **Old Harbour Office**, now HM Coastguard and Fisheries. This building until recently housed the office of the Poole Harbour Commissioners. The present building dates from 1822, and used to be known as the Town House. It replaced a former Town House on the same site which dated from 1727. There is a plaque on the gable end, facing into Thames Street, which contains a coloured bas-relief of Benjamin Skutt, who was Mayor of the town in 1727, and in the centre of the front wall is a sundial dated 1814 - both these being remains from the earlier town house.

Old Harbour Office - seen from the Quay with the Staplecross to the right and a huge grain warehouse looming behind. The neat colonnaded building dates from 1822 but has a 1727 bas-relief of Mayor Benjamin Skutt and a sundail of 1814 (both pictured overleaf).

The building's original purpose was "for the convenience of merchants and others, as a news room and place of general resort ". All the leading London newspapers and periodicals were provided, and with its prime quayside situation, it must formerly have been a place of much activity, gossip, and commerce.

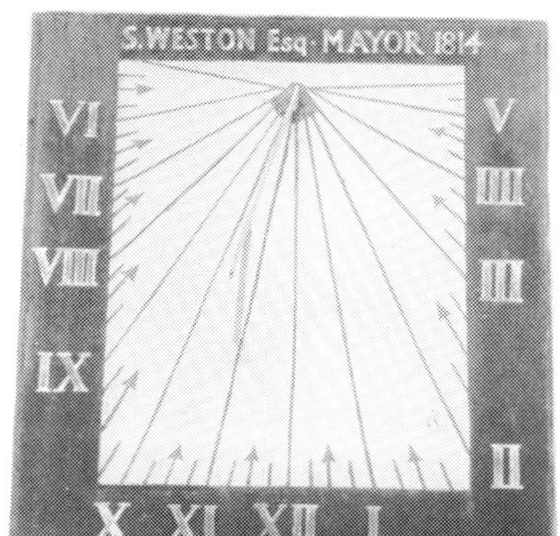

The Custom House - with the Staplecross in the foreground.
The building is a replica of that destroyed by fire in 1813.
Similarly the Stapecross is a replica of the Town Beam of 1433.

Here you will see also the **Customs House** and **Staplecross** or **Town Beam**. The Staplecross or Town Beam is - as the inscription records - a replica of a much earlier structure. Similarly, the Customs House is itself a replica of two much earlier buildings.

Towards the end of the eighteenth century, a Customs House was built on this site which was a copy of a much earlier building, then the Red Lion Coffee House. But the first Customs House was burned down in 1813, and the present building was erected in the same year, as a replica of it. So today's Custom House is in fact a copy not only of an earlier building, but of the building preceding that.

Similarly, the Staplecross or Town Beam is a replica of a much earlier Beam dating initially from about 1433, the year in which Poole was created a Port of the Staple - hence the Beam's being known also as the Staplecross. The inscription on

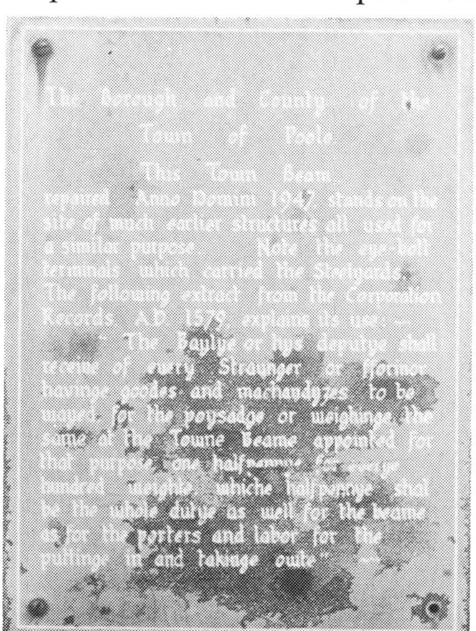

the Beam explains its purpose: "The Baylye or hys Deputye shall receive of every Straunger or fforinor havinge goodes and machendyzes to be wayed, for the poysadge or weighinge the same at the Town Beame appointed for that purpose one halfpennye for everye hundred weighte, which halfpennye shal be the whole dutye as well for the beame as for the porters and labor for the puttinge in and takinge oute."

The present Beam was erected in 1947–obviously a bad year for the apostrophe!

On the quayside opposite the Custom House you will see the **Custom House Steps.** It is from these steps each year that the "Admiral of the Port of Poole" sets sail, together with other local dignitaries in the ceremony known as the "beating of the water bounds", journeying to certain points in the harbour to confirm the Mayor's jurisdiction over the water boundaries of the harbour.

The custom of the beating of the bounds dates from the granting to the town of the Winchelsea Certificate in 1364. The Longspee Charter of 1241 had established the role of Port-Reeve with authority as the Admiral of the Port and leader of the Admiralty Court, which could decide on legal problems to do with shipping and customs duty being brought into the harbour.

But there had been some confusion over the extent of the Port-Reeve's authority and Winchelsea, one of the Cinque Ports and a self-appointed arbiter in matters to do with maritime law, had been asked to step in to clarify the situation. The Winchelsea Certificate confirmed the Port-Reeve's authority as Admiral of the Port and leader of the Admiralty Court, and this was upheld a few years later by the Montacute Charter of 1371, which changed the title of Port-Reeve to Mayor. Over six hundred years later, the Mayor of Poole still sets out from the Bounds Steps to confirm the rights of the Winchelsea Certificate.

Walk along the quay towards Poole Bridge, leaving the Old Harbour Office on your right. After about 100 yards you pass **Yeatman's Old Mill,** built about 1790. Immediately adjacent to the Old Mill you turn into a narrow alley, **St Clements Lane.**

You are now walking towards **Watergate**. There has always been considerable controversy about this short section of wall. Many local people believe it to be the last remaining section of the old town wall, dating from the early medieval period, and this is a view supported by several early, eminent historians of Poole and Dorset, such as Leland, Hutchins, and Sydenham: "A wall was also erected on the seaward side of the town which, we are told by Leland, was commenced by Richard III. Of this, at the time in which the topographer wrote, there were remaining but a small embattled gate and some of an embattled wall."

There is, however, little or no evidence to suggest that a town wall as such was ever built as the town relied for its landward defence on the tidal bog which ran from about Towngate Bridge through to Parkstone Bay and which was cut through sometime in the 1400s. Furthermore, excavation around the wall has shown that the water's edge at one time came up to this point, and so it seems more likely that what we now see was instead a water-gate giving access to the shore from a mansion in Thames Street.

Whatever the case, this wall - which is between eighteen inches and three feet thick, and runs for about fifteen yards - is a fairly substantial structure, and it is a little difficult to conceive of it as a mere garden wall. The notion that it is part of the town's defences - if not historically accurate - is

certainly more in accord with most people's sense of the past. The truth is probably a mixture of the two.

The Watergate - ancient looks but doubted antiquity, despite the corbel-table that projects along the right-hand wall.

Continue through St Clements Lane with its twists and turns. This will return you to **Thames Street.** Turn left towards St James's Church. Immediately on your left is the **Mansion House**.

This is one of the finest examples of the great Georgian mansions built when the Newfoundland trade was at its height. It was begun in 1776 by Isaac Lester, but he died in 1778 and the building was completed by his brother Benjamin.

It was Benjamin - a much less dour man than his high-minded brother - who added a further storey and other decorations to the house. The most famous of his decorative touches are the two fillets of dried cod sculpted into the frieze of the dining-room fireplace as a permanent reminder of the source of the family's fortunes. Benjamin Lester became MP for Poole in 1790, and died in 1802, one of the great characters of the town and of his age.

The Mansion House has been the home over the years for two of the most powerful of the Newfoundland trading families, the Lesters, and later the Garlands. Despite various upheavals, and even a period in which the building almost fell derelict, it has been recently restored to its former grandeur and is now a private dining club.

The Mansion House - Georgian grandeur for the Lester brothers.

Poole House - built by the Weston family about 1730. It was later owned by the Slade family. They prospered on the town's deep-water fish trade, across the Atlantic to the Newfoundland Banks, the proceeds of which were generally transforming mediaeval Poole into a Georgian new town.

Walking along Thames Street and towards St James's Church, you will notice several quite impressive Georgian Mansions. The most impressive are **Poole House** and **West End House**, and there is, in fact, an interesting connection between them.

Poole House was built about 1730 by the Weston family, a family which provided Poole with many of its mayors throughout the eighteenth century. The house later passed into the Slade family, who were Newfoundland traders and built West End House at the end of Thames Street. Note the four stone urns and pineapples surmounting the facade of West End House - symbols of the extravagance of the lifestyle of many of the Newfoundland traders of the period.

At **St James's Church** you are at the centre of the old town. Religious worship has taken place on this site since the twelfth century, and for many of the townsfolk of Poole their baptism, marriage, and burial services would all have been held

West End House - more Slade family pineapples top the facade.

St James's church - rebuilt in 1820.

at this spot. The Church was granted the status of "Royal Peculiar" in the sixteenth century, giving certain exemptions from the authority of the Bishop, and the Choristers of St James's still wear red cassocks to mark this Royal favour.

The present Georgian Gothic building was erected in 1820, at a cost of £11,740. If the Church is open, you may wish to visit the interior; there is a fine stained-glass east window, and you will also notice that the vaulted roof is supported by pine columns. It has been suggested that these were brought back by ships involved in the Newfoundland trade. Hanging from one of the pillars is a Union Jack which was the first flag to be flown over liberated Paris by the Allies in 1944.

Follow the path around the perimeter of the Church. As you pass beside the Church into St. James's Close, you will see on your left an enclosed grassy area. The yew tree which flourishes here is traditionally associated with graveyards, and this land is in fact a now-disused "Burying Ground" opened in 1773 when the space around the Church became full. Note the headstone set into the wall of the house on the left.

Ahead and to the left stands the **Rectory,** built in 1786 by the merchants of Poole Corporation. It is a two-storey building with cellars and attics, elegantly designed in a five bay frontage with a central doorway and fanlight. The original iron railings survive, enclosing the front garden.

The Rectory - 1786 elegance.

Market Street - imposing doors.

The Almshouses - mediaeval but with a commemorative tablet added in 1904.

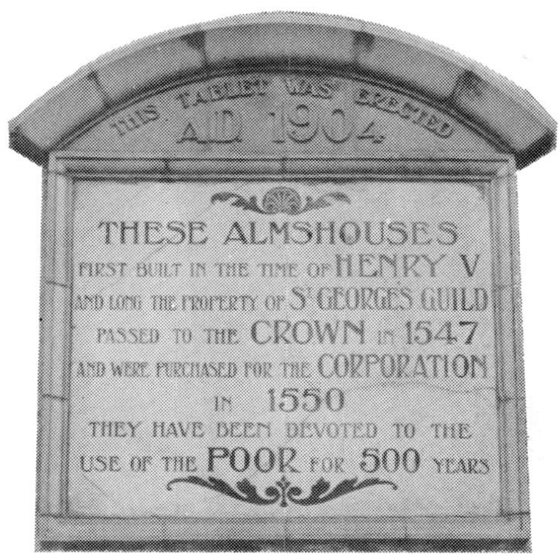

Continue to the end of **Rectory Walk** and turn left, away from the Church into **Market Street**. As you walk along Market Street you will see many fine examples of eighteenth century town houses, with their imposing doors and door surrounds. Much older than these, however, about thirty yards on your right-hand side, are the town's medieval **Almshouses.**

Originally built sometime in the 1400s, the Almshouses have been considerably altered over the years. The Almshouses were established and paid for by the Fraternity of St George, a religious Guild founded about 1400, and until 1550 provided homes for the priests of St James's Church.

In 1550, as the plaque on the Market Street wall records, the

Almshouses were purchased from the Crown by Poole Corporation. It was about this time - or slightly later - that most of the rebuilding took place, the Almshouses thereafter being used exclusively to house the old and the poor of the town.

Street lighting - niche for an oil-lamp.

As you approach the Almshouses, along Church Street, you will notice a small oval niche in the end wall of the building. This niche originally held an oil-lamp, and provided the town with its first primitive street-lighting.

On your left about twenty yards past the Almshouses stands **Byngley House.** This property was originally a larger town house, incorporating its neighbour, number eight. It was built by Thomas Byngley, Mayor of Poole in 1567. The front wall and chimney stacks were of stone, but the rear walls were of timber-framed construction, an interesting mix of two building styles. In the mid eighteenth century the house was divided into two separate dwellings, and the original front doorway replaced by the present pair of doorways. Local tradition has it that Oliver Cromwell lodged in Byngley House during the siege of Corfe Castle - not that history records any such personal appearance in the local skirmishes.

As you continue along Market Street towards the Guildhall, you will see on your left another fine example of a Georgian mansion, further evidence of the town's prosperity during the years of the Newfoundland trade.

Opposite:
Byngley House - built by Poole's mayor in 1567. Since split into two dwellings, but retaining something of its stone frontage to Church Street.

The Angel - mail coaches to the capital.

On your left as you approach the Guildhall, you will see the **Angel Inn**. This coaching inn was built in the eighteenth century, and mail coaches left here daily for London. The large archway and gate allowed the coach and horses to proceed directly to the inner courtyard.

Immediately ahead of you is the imposing eighteenth century **Guildhall**. The building of the Guildhall began in 1761, as is recorded on the plaque on the Market Street wall, half the cost of building being provided by the town's two MPs, Thomas Calcraft and Joseph Gulston.

Guildhall plaque - commemorates the munificent MPs of 1761.

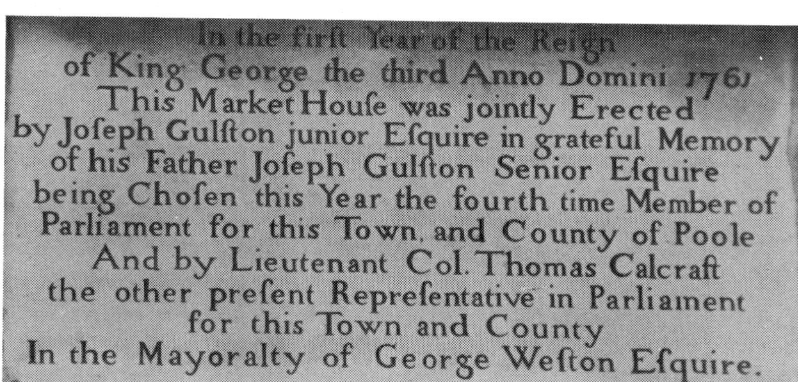

Guildhall - seen from Market Street, in its full Georgian splendour. The backdrop of terraced cottages was swept away in the 1960s for roads and car-parks. Drawn by Sheila Sturdy.

The Guildhall replaced the previous building in Fish Street, which had also contained the town prison, described at the time as "a loathsome, crumbling building", and from which in 1777 the Keeper of the Gaol was sacked for "suffering it to be used as a common bawdy house."

The present imposing building is in two storeys. The ground floor was originally open at the Market Street end and served as a busy market until the mid-nineteenth century. The principal room of the upper floor was once the Council Chamber and was used for all meetings of the Corporation and Town Council until the new Municipal Building at Park Gates was built in 1932. This room was also used for the Poole Quarter Sessions and Magistrates' Courts.

Many of the townsfolk will have had their fate decided in this room. In 1842, for instance, George Cookman was sentenced "to be transported to such place beyond the seas as Her Majesty ....shall direct."

The building was also used from 1819–1821 as the Parish Church while St James's was demolished and a replacement erected.

During the Second World War, the American Red Cross and American soldiers preparing for D-Day used the building as a canteen and recreation centre. The Mayor of the town later received a letter from the Lady Commandant of the American Red Cross thanking the town for the use of "Ye olde Ancient Monument" - by which she meant the Guildhall.

It is now one of Poole's three museums, and houses an interesting collection of exhibits relating to the history of the town. There is a fascinating collection of local documents, plans, and maps, a short audio-visual presentation, and usually one or two visiting exhibitions. It is well worth a visit to conclude your walk around the historic town of Poole.

The multi-storey car park with your car lies directly ahead, across the main road. Unfortunately, this modern car park has no historical connections and little architectural merit...........

Opposite:
Alley off Thames Street - Georgian brick and tile, cobbles, and early 20th century gas-lamp cast with the town's dolphin logo. Photographed by Rodney Legg.

REFERENCES AND FURTHER READING

Derek Beamish et al	*Mansions and Merchants of Poole and Dorset* 1976
Cecil Cullingford	*A History of Dorset* 1980
John Hutchins	*The History and Antiquities of the County of Dorset* Vol. 1 (1774)
A.J. Miller	*The Story of Poole* 1984
John Sydenham	*History of the Town and County of Poole* 1839, reprinted 1976